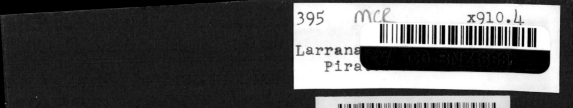

pirates and

buccaneers

Walking the Plank, a drawing by American artist Howard Pyle (1853-1911), who illustrated many tales of piracy and adventure.

A Pull Ahead Book

pirates and
buccaneers

Robert D. Larranaga

Lerner Publications Company • Minneapolis, Minnesota

ACKNOWLEDGMENTS: The illustrations are reproduced through the courtesy of: pp. 2, 20, 24, 25, 28, 30, 33, 34, 37, 39, 40, 42, 47, 52, The New York Public Library; pp. 5, 13, 22, 27, 49, 57, Delaware Art Center, Wilmington (Howard Pyle Collection); pp. 6, 59, Culver Pictures, Inc.; pp. 8-9, 15, 44, National Maritime Museum, Greenwich, England; pp. 12, 53, Library of Congress; p. 16, City Art Gallery, Plymouth, England; p. 45, Robert I. Nesmith, *Dig for Pirate Treasure*, The Devin-Adair Company.

Front cover: Pirates Attacking and Boarding a Ship, Radio Times Hulton Picture Library, London.

Back cover: Blackbeard's Last Fight by Howard Pyle, Delaware Art Center, Wilmington (Howard Pyle Collection).

Standard Book Number: 8225-0458-8
Library of Congress Catalog Card Number: 74-84412

Captain Kidd

contents

The Vikings were great sailors and shipbuilders of the early Middle Ages. They raided coastal towns all over Europe and even sailed up the rivers to plunder towns far from the sea.

Pirates of the Past

Pirate tales have been told for as long as men have gone to sea. In the days of Greece and Rome, pirates roamed the Mediterranean Sea in slave-driven galleys armed with fearful weapons. Catapults heaved basketfuls of poisonous snakes aboard other ships. Buckets hanging from the yardarm poured boiling oil on the enemy deck. It took a fleet of 270 Roman ships to defeat these pirates in 67 B.C.

In the seventh century A.D., fierce pirates dressed in animal skins, breastplates, and winged helmets swept out of the North. In dragon-prowed "longships," these Vikings raided Britain, France, and Italy. For the next 200 years Europe trembled to their war cry, "Ahoy!"

Meanwhile, a new breed of pirate had appeared on the Mediterranean. Corsairs from Africa's Barbary Coast attacked spice ships returning from the Orient. First Italy, and then Spain, tried to crush them. Yet the corsairs grew stronger and bolder under Khair ad-Din Barbarossa, a red-bearded Algerian. In 1533 Barbarossa retired from piracy, undefeated, to become head of the Turkish navy.

Now, halfway around the world, the golden age of piracy was about to begin.

Spain and Portugal had discovered fabulous treasures in the New World. Special ships were built to carry this precious cargo — high-sided galleons, with three masts, three decks, and many cannon. Into these ships went 75-pound bars of silver, 40-pound bars of gold, crude coins made right on the spot, emeralds, pearls, indigo, and tobacco.

Word of these treasures spread throughout Europe, and soon pirates and privateers (pirates licensed by a king who shared the booty) set sail for the West Indies.

Small, swift English ships capture a Spanish treasure galleon (center), 1628. The galleon is loaded with silver from Peru.

Sailors lucky enough to return safely from the New World told tales of men like Francis "the Dragon" Drake, Bartolomey the Portuguese, L'Olonnois "the Cruel," Henry Morgan, Blackbeard, and Captain Kidd. These are just a few of the great pirates whose lives you'll read about in this book.

NORTH AMERICA

Atlantic Ocean

PAMLICO SOUND

CHARLESTON

BARATARIA

NEW ORLEANS

ST. AUGUSTINE

GALVESTON ISLAND

Gulf of Mexico

BAHAMA ISLANDS

CUBA

ZACATECAS

VERA CRUZ

Gulf of Campeche

CAMPECHE

GUANAJUATO

TORTUGA (ILE DE LA TORTUE)

HISPANIOLA

JAMAICA

HAITI

DOMINICAN REPUBLIC

VIRGIN ISLANDS

PORT ROYAL

PORT AU PRINCE

SANTO DOMINGO

BARBADOS ISLAND

MARTINIQUE

CENTRAL AMERICA

Caribbean Sea

CARTAGENA

Gulfo Triste

PORTO BELLO

MARACAIBO

PUERTO CABELLO

NOMBRE DE DIOS

PANAMA CITY

GIBRALTAR

VENEZUELA

GUYANA

COLUMBIA

ECUADOR

BRAZIL

PERU

Pacific Ocean

LIMA

HUANCAVELICA

BOLIVIA

ARICA

POTOSI

CHILE

The Spanish Main. Spain's most productive mining centers were Guanajuato and Zacatecas in Mexico, and the Peruvian towns of Huancavelica and Potosi (now in Bolivia). Every year two fleets of galleons left Spain for the New World; one fleet sailed to Cartagena and Porto Bello to collect South American treasure, then to Havana where it met the other fleet bearing gold and silver from Mexico. Together the galleons sailed back to Spain — if they were able to evade the pirates lurking in Caribbean waters.

Sir Francis Drake

Francis Drake grew up on the waterfront. His family was so poor that for a while they lived in a wrecked ship in Plymouth harbor, England. At 15, he shipped aboard a coastal sloop as a crew of one for an old sea captain. When the old man died a few years later, he left his boat to Drake. Francis sold the boat, and joined a fleet of slave ships sailing for Africa and the New World under his kinsman, Sir John Hawkins.

The voyage was a disaster. A fleet of 13 Spanish men-o-war attacked the illegal slave ships outside of Vera Cruz, Mexico. Only two ships escaped: the *Minion* under Hawkins, and the *Judith* under Drake.

But Drake had had a glimpse of the New World's fabled treasures. Within three years, towns up and down the Spanish Main spoke of "El Draque" in fearful tones. With two ships, the *Pasha* and the *Swan*, 73 men, and a letter of marque (a license) from Queen Elizabeth, he had become an English privateer.

Sir Francis Drake (1540?-1596)

Drake wasn't satisfied with raiding ships. In 1572, he attacked the great treasure storehouse at the town of Nombre de Dios (NOM-bray day dee-OS) in Panama. The pirates were met by a hail of bullets. Drake lashed out with his cutlass ("Attack, you seadogs, attack!") and drove his men to the very gates of the storehouse. Then a lucky bullet hit him in the leg, and his men had to retreat with their wounded leader.

"Next time," Drake said, "we'll ambush the pack train from Potosi before it reaches town with the silver."

Joining forces with some Indians and a French pirate named le Testu, he ambushed a pack train carrying 30 tons of silver ingots. The battle was short and bloody. Drake returned victorious to England where he had no trouble finding backers for his next adventure.

Drake's Attack Upon Santo Domingo, a painting by Howard Pyle. In his 1585 campaign Drake took little plunder and lost many men.

The Spanish Armada, detail of design for a tapestry. The defeat of the Armada in 1588 marked a turning point in Spanish and English sea power; Spain's control of the New World gradually declined, and England's rose.

He set out with five ships to plunder the poorly defended towns on the Pacific coast of South America. Four of the ships were lost, but Drake continued on in the *Golden Hind*, robbing an entire Spanish fleet at Lima, sacking the city, seizing a pack train, and taking the city of Arica.

He returned home in 1580 by way of the Cape of Good Hope to become the second man in history to sail around the world. The three-year trip had earned Drake $100,000. Spain screamed for his head. England knighted him.

"My dear pyrat," Queen Elizabeth said, "we do account that he which striketh at thee, striketh at us."

In 1585, the Queen helped equip Drake with the largest English fleet to ever set sail for the New World — 25 ships, 2,500 men. His mission was to weaken Spain before she decided to declare war on England. But this time Drake was not so lucky.

He captured the cities of Santo Domingo, Cartagena, and St. Augustine, but took very little plunder — the Spanish had been warned of his coming, and had hidden their treasure. What's more, Drake paid a fearful toll for his victories. Over one-third of his men had died either in battle or of yellow fever. The Queen was displeased with him.

Spain was enraged. Shortly after Drake's return, the Spanish Armada — a fleet of 130 ships — attacked England.

Drake was buried at sea near Nombre de Dios, Panama, on January 28, 1596.

The battle was to be Drake's finest hour. Using every pirate trick he had learned, he spearheaded the smaller English fleet. He out-maneuvered the larger Spanish galleons, scattered them with "fireships" (ships covered with pitch, tar, and explosives and set afire) and then attacked isolated galleons. The battle lasted two days with neither side gaining the upper hand until a storm came up and destroyed much of the Spanish fleet.

Drake was a national hero again. But court life did not agree with the boy who had grown up on the waterfront. He returned to the Caribbean where he continued to plunder Spanish ships and cities until he died of a fever at sea in 1596.

Drake's daring exploits set the stage for a new era in piracy: the era of the buccaneer.

Ships much like this galleon were used by most European nations in the 16th and 17th centuries.

The Buccaneers

The year was 1665. A large Spanish galleon cut through the waters off the coast of Hispaniola (now Haiti and the Dominican Republic), her holds weighed down with treasure from the New World, her gunports bristling with cannon.

"Ship ahoy!" came the cry from the topsail.

In the distance, a small open boat was approaching. Fearing pirates, several crewmen asked for permission to sink her. But the captain felt the small boat was harmless, and ordered his men to drop anchor for the night.

Now, under cover of darkness, the smaller boat headed silently for the galleon. Once alongside, her captain had two holes drilled in the bottom of his own boat. "Once we go over the side," he explained to his men, "I don't want anyone retreating." With cutlasses drawn and pistols cocked, the pirates scrambled up the side of the galleon.

"Sea demons!" the Spanish cried, for they had not seen any boats approaching. They fled to the forecastle without firing a shot.

The ship's captain was still playing cards when his cabin door was kicked open, and the pirate chieftain stepped in.

"I, Pierre le Grand, have taken command of this ship," he roared. And a very special ship it was. It belonged to the vice admiral of the fleet, and contained enough treasure to enable Pierre and his men to retire in luxury.

When word of this feat reached the islands of Tortuga and Hispaniola, it changed the course of history. Until then, the buccaneers had limited themselves to rustling cattle and selling the dried beef to passing ships ("buccaneer" comes from the French word for "drier of beef"). But it was clear that more money could be made at pirating.

The buccaneers formed a group called the Brethren of the Coast, which followed the pirate code. This code — known as the Jamaica Discipline — helped determine who was to be captain of a ship, how the booty was to be split, and so on. For instance, a captain's share of the booty was usually six times greater than a crewman's; the first mate's was twice as great; and the injured received extra portions. The loss of a right arm entitled a buccaneer to around 600 extra pieces of eight; the loss of a left arm was worth 500. If one buccaneer stole from another, his ears and nose were cut off; if he was caught a second time, he would be marooned on a desert island with a musket, ammunition, and a bottle of water.

The buccaneers reached the peak of their power in the late 1600's when they had strongholds on Tortuga, Hispaniola, the Virgin Islands, and Jamaica.

Pierre le Grand, French buccaneer (center), directs the capture of a Spanish galleon.

Marooned, a painting by Howard Pyle. A buccaneer
who broke the rules is left alone on a barren island.

Bartolomey the Portuguese

One of the earliest buccaneers was Bartolomey the Portuguese. Declaring himself a pirate, he set out in a small boat to duplicate the feat of Pierre le Grand. His ship had only four cannon but he attacked a ship with 24.

The cunning pirate out-sailed the larger ship, avoiding its cannon for three hours, while his riflemen picked off every Spaniard who raised his head above the gunwale.

When the Spaniards were weakened, the pirates tried to board. The second time they gained the deck, but the defenders fought on. When the battle finally ended, Bartolomey had only 15 pirates left to sail his prize.

They headed for Jamaica as fast as possible. It wasn't fast enough. Three Spanish men-o-war overtook and captured the pirates. Soon Bartolomey found himself imprisoned below deck on a ship in Campeche (cam-PAY-chay) harbor, Mexico, waiting to be hanged.

A guard stood outside his cell. A hundred yards of water stood between him and safety, and Bartolomey couldn't swim. Yet he managed to escape. That night, when the guard brought his supper, Bartolomey overpowered him, and dove overboard with two large air-tight jugs for life preservers. By the time his escape was noticed, he had made the shore and was on his way to Golfo Triste (GOL-fo TREES-tay), Venezuela.

Bartolomey the Portuguese

It took him two weeks to cover the 120 miles, and every step of the way, Bartolomey planned his revenge. In Golfo Triste, he gathered a new pirate crew for an attack on the very ship that had captured him. The unsuspecting ship was still anchored at Campeche when Bartolomey's men swarmed over the sides, catching the crew below decks. Before anyone in the harbor could stop them, the pirates had weighed anchor and set sail.

But their victory was short-lived. A tremendous storm caught Bartolomey's ship off Pinos Island, and all aboard died in the wreckage.

Roc Brasiliano

Roc Brasiliano

About this time, in the 1660's, Roc Brasiliano became pirate chief of Jamaica. He had been driven from his plantation in Brazil by the Spaniards, and sought revenge on the high seas by sinking Spanish galleons.

Roc was a barrel-chested bulldog of a man who loved a good fight. He walked the streets of Jamaica with a scowl on his face and a sword in his hand. Every pirate on the island feared him. He soon became drunk with power.

His crew swarming about him, a pirate captain demands that towns-people hand over their gold. If his request is denied, the pirates will sack and burn the town. (Painting by Howard Pyle)

When he dared to sail into Campeche harbor in a small open boat, he was arrested. Once in jail, Roc began plotting his escape. He wrote a note in French to the governor of Campeche demanding his release. Then he bribed a Negro slave to deliver it and claim the note came from the captain of the French ship riding anchor in the harbor.

The governor believed the note was from the French captain, and fearing he would open fire on the city with his cannon, he freed the pirates. Roc was forced to travel to Spain with the other pardoned pirates, but he soon returned to Jamaica.

Next, he joined forces with the French buccaneer, Tributor. Together they attacked Merida, Yucatan. As the pirates charged the fort, they were attacked from behind by horsemen. The ambush worked. Roc and a few of his crew fled, leaving the others to be massacred on the beach.

But when Roc reached Jamaica, the other buccaneers would have nothing to do with him. In their eyes, only cowards retreated. Roc was no longer their leader.

L'Olonnois (1630?-1671), French corsair

L'Olonnois

The worst cutthroat of all was Jean-David Nau, known as L'Olonnois (low-lun-wah) the Cruel.

Nau was born in 1630 in the French town of Sables l'Olonne. At the age of 20 he went to the West Indies as an indentured servant, but was soon captain of a French corsair ship that flew two flags — the Jolly Roger, and the red flag which signified "no quarter given." L'Olonnois thought nothing of torturing his victims.

He ravaged Spanish shipping for years until a storm wrecked his ship near Campeche. Suddenly soldiers from the town attacked the pirates. L'Olonnois, fearing he would be captured, bloodied his clothes and pretended to be dead. The battle raged on about him, but L'Olonnois didn't budge; when the last pirate had been captured, the Spaniards returned to town without him.

That night there was singing and dancing in the streets of Campeche: L'Olonnois was dead! No one noticed the shadowy figure who slipped down to the dock, climbed into a boat, and sailed off in the darkness.

When the governor of Cuba learned of L'Olonnois's escape, he sent a man-o-war after the pirate. Their orders: bring L'Olonnois back hanging by his neck from the yardarm.

By this time L'Olonnois had a new ship and a new crew. He was itching for a fight. Instead of retreating, he laid a trap for the man-o-war.

Seizing a Spanish fishing boat, he sailed for the man-o-war. The two ships met near the Cuban village of De Los Cayos. Darkness was falling when a lookout on the man-o-war hailed the fishing vessel. At knife-point, L'Olonnois ordered one of his prisoners to reply in Spanish.

L'Olonnois gouges out the heart of a Spanish prisoner and waves it in the face of another.

The two ships drew closer and closer. Suddenly they were side by side, and pirates were swarming on the decks of the man-o-war. Most of the crew was caught below deck. The ship was his, but L'Olonnois wasn't satisfied. In a rage, he ordered the Spaniards to be brought on deck one by one. Then, with his cutlass, he beheaded 90 of them. The last man was saved.

"Tell your governor what you've seen," the pirate roared, "and let this be a warning to him."

In 1667, the bloodthirsty L'Olonnois sacked the cities of Maracaibo (mar-eh-KY-bo) and Gibraltar, in Venezuela. But the booty was soon spent, and he took to sea again. This time he captured Puerto Cabello (pwert-o keh-BAY-yo), Venezuela. It was to be L'Olonnois's last victory.

Near Las Perlas Island he was attacked by a large Spanish fleet. In a fierce running battle he fought his way to the coast of Cartagena, where he and a few of his men escaped. But not for long. They were caught by the fierce Carib Indians and met a horrible death.

Henry Morgan

The greatest buccaneer of all time was Morgan "the Terrible."

Henry Morgan was a Welsh farm boy who ran away to sea. Arriving at Barbados Island without any money, he was sold to a plantation owner. To get out of bondage Morgan enlisted in the British army at the age of 20. After his discharge, he joined with some other ex-soldiers in buying a privateering ship.

By 1666, he had risen to vice admiral of a fleet of 15 ships. Under the old buccaneer Mansveldt, the fleet sailed to the island of Santa Catalina near Costo Rica. They took the island but very little booty. The buccaneers fought among themselves. Mansveldt sailed for Tortuga alone and Morgan took command of the fleet.

His first major attack, in 1668, was against the inland city of Puerto Principe (pwert-o PREEN-the-pay), Cuba. The pirates were ambushed along the way, and took the city only after a bitter struggle. To make matters worse, most of the city's treasure had been hidden. The buccaneers had to settle for 50,000 pieces of eight in return for sparing their captives.

Sir Henry Morgan
(1635?-1688)

Half his men quit after Puerto Principe. Yet Morgan was undaunted. Returning to Port Royal, Jamaica, he announced plans for attacking the great treasure city of Porto Bello, Panama. The older sea dogs scoffed at his plan. Porto Bello was larger than Puerto Principe, and was defended by three heavily armed forts, and an army troop.

"Morgan won't stand a chance," they said.

Imagine their surprise when Morgan not only attacked Porto Bello, but arrived in canoes instead of ships. Hugging the shoreline, under cover of darkness, his men slipped into the harbor before the city fathers knew they were there.

At Porto Bello, Morgan's men storm the walls of the last fort. The governor himself defended the fort, directing his troops to pour fire on the pirates.

The first two forts fell in quick succession, but the third withstood every attack until Morgan came up with a fiendish plan: he used captured priests and nuns to shield his men as they scaled the walls of the fort. Within a few hours the city fell into his hands along with 250,000 pieces of eight and 300 slaves.

Word of this feat spread throughout the Caribbean, and Morgan's force swelled to 15 ships and 900 men.

Next he attacked the Venezuelan cities of Maracaibo and Gibraltar. Maracaibo is a coastal city located at the mouth of an inland lake and guarded by an island fortress. Gibraltar is at the other end of the lake. Morgan found both cities virtually deserted, but managed to fill his treasure chest after torturing a few captives.

When the pirates tried to sail out of the lake, they found their exit blocked. The guns of Maracaibo's fort were trained on them and three huge Spanish men-o-war stood just outside the channel. Morgan immediately sent a note demanding their surrender. The Spaniards laughed. The pirate decided to teach them a lesson.

He had his lead ship, a small sloop, covered with pitch, tar, brimstone, and gunpowder. Then he had dummies (made of kegs and pumpkins, and dressed to look like buccaneers) placed at battle stations throughout the ship. The Spaniards were still laughing when the small ship attacked them. Suddenly it burst into flames and exploded, sinking the first man-o-war. The second went aground trying to escape, and burned to the hull. The third was easily captured by the pirates.

Once again Morgan demanded the fort's surrender. Once again they refused. With a shrug of his shoulders Morgan ordered his longboats to embark for shore. A jetty blocked their view, but the men in the fort saw enough to think the pirates were massing for a land attack. They moved their cannon to the other side of the fort. That night — before the cannon could be moved again — Morgan sailed safely past the fort. Only then did the Spaniards realize they'd been tricked. Instead of landing on the other side of the jetty, the crews of the longboats had simply crouched below the gunwale and returned to their ships.

Morgan was now undisputed king of the buccaneers. And for his next target he chose a king's ransom, the gold of Panama City. In 1670 he set sail with 40 ships and 2,000 men. After seizing Fort San Lorenzo at the mouth of the Chagres River, he anchored his ships and made a brutal 16-day trip by boat and foot across the steaming isthmus of Panama. The Spaniards knew of his attack and were ready.

"*Viva el Rey*," they cried, "Long live the King!"

Morgan captures Fort San Lorenzo on his
way to Panama City. December 27, 1670.

Six hundred cavalry swooped down on Morgan's men. A thousand muskets fired; the buccaneers held their ground. Then a herd of 2,000 Spanish bulls were stampeded right at them.

"Shoot at the lead bulls," Morgan yelled, and again the pirates fired. The herd swerved away, and the pirates began their advance. The Spanish infantry fired a few shots, threw down their muskets, and fled. The city belonged to the buccaneers.

Unfortunately for Morgan, England had just signed a treaty with Spain, and Panama City was no longer fair game. When he returned to Jamaica he was put in chains and shipped to England to stand trial as a pirate. King Charles II learned of Morgan's great deeds, however, and decided to make better use of his talents. He knighted Morgan in 1673 and made him lieutenant governor of Jamaica with orders to rid the seas of the buccaneers.

Morgan did a complete about-face and for the rest of his life he was the scourge of all buccaneers. Often he hanged men who had sailed under him. When he died in 1688, there were only a few buccaneers left. He had done his job well.

Corsairs boarding a Spanish vessel by moonlight.

Anne Bonny and Mary Read were convicted of piracy in 1720 at a court in Port Royal, Jamaica. Mary, an ex-soldier in the British army, had sailed to the West Indies on a Dutch ship. Captured by pirates, she joined their crew, and later fell in with Calico Jack Rackham and Anne Bonny. Mary was sentenced to hang, but she died of a fever; though Anne was spared the gallows her fate is unknown.

Pirates of the Atlantic

Many of the buccaneers spread out from the Caribbean into the waters of the Atlantic where they were labelled "pirates." For the next 100 years, American shipping was threatened by a motley crew of cutthroats.

There was Stede Bonnet, a retired army major, who became bored with farming, and took up piracy in 1717 only to be caught and hanged within the year.

There was Bartholomew Roberts, the gentleman pirate, who didn't allow drinking or gambling on his ship, and never fought on Sunday; yet he captured 400 ships — more than any other Atlantic pirate.

There was Ned Low, a madman who was so cruel his own crew set him adrift in an open boat without food, water, or weapons. He was picked up by a passing boat and taken to the island of Martinique where he was hanged.

There were even a few women pirates. Two of them, Anne Bonny and Mary Read, pretended to be men, and sailed together under Calico Jack Rackham. Once Mary Read fought a duel with a pirate who had insulted her "secret" lover. She shot the man and then ran him through with her sword.

Among all the pirates of this period, three stand out: Captain Kidd, Long Ben Avery, and Blackbeard.

Captain Kidd (1645?-1701) on the deck
of the *Adventure Galley.* (Painting by
Howard Pyle)

Captain Kidd

The most famous pirate of all time was Captain Kidd,
who had originally set out to rid the seas of pirates.

Born in about 1645, Kidd was an English privateer who
was so successful in the West Indies and New York that he
was called back to England in 1695. Several officers of the
King asked him to captain the *Adventure Galley*, a new ship
with 34 cannon and a crew of 80. Its mission: to capture all
French ships, and the pirates of Madagascar, especially
"Thomas Tew, John Ireland, Captain Thomas Wales, Captain William Maze . . . "

Kidd accepted. But after fighting a French ship in mid-
Atlantic, he decided he needed a better crew. He recruited a
gang of cutthroats in New York, and set sail for Madagascar.

Once there, many of his crew jumped ship to join the
pirates. The others threatened mutiny unless Kidd attacked
any and all ships. He refused. A fight broke out between
Kidd and one of his gunners, and he killed the man.

After that Kidd was a changed man, menacing shipping all along India's Malabar coast. The holds of the *Adventure Galley* were already loaded with booty when Kidd spied the sails of the *Quedagh Merchant,* a huge treasure ship of 400 tons (the *Adventure Galley* weighed only 284 tons).

The pirates gave chase, crowding all sail to the wind. A cannonball splashed across the bow of the *Quedagh Merchant* — the signal to surrender — but her captain ordered his men to prepare for battle. Sailors scurried up the shrouds to trim the sails; below decks men opened powder kegs and filled water buckets for fire fighting; others dropped wet blankets across the sides to guard against splinters, and spread sand on the deck for better footing.

(Left) Captain Kidd flings a bucket at William Moore, his gunner. Moore died of the blow, and five years later Kidd was tried for his murder, as well as on several counts of piracy.

Battle of Vigo Bay, October 1702. The year after Kidd's death, British and Dutch ships attacked a huge Spanish treasure fleet hiding in Vigo Bay off northwest Spain. They sank all the ships but a few special prizes. The rest of the treasure still lies at the bottom of Vigo Bay.

With the pirates closing in, the *Quedagh Merchant* fired a broadside. But a sudden ocean swell caused the shots to miss their mark and before she could reload, grappling hooks had lashed the ships together.

Pirates poured over the side. Smoke filled the air, the decks ran red, and soon Captain Kidd took possession of one of the greatest pirate treasures ever — his share alone was worth $60,000!

Now, standing on the deck of the *Quedagh Merchant*, he ordered his crew to set sail for New York. Kidd thought he could fool the New Yorkers into believing all his booty had been taken from French and pirate ships. He was mistaken. Much of the booty belonged to the powerful British East India Company. They had Kidd clapped into chains and shipped to England where he was sentenced to death.

Kidd met a horrible end. The hangman's rope broke twice. The third time it held, and afterwards his body was cut down, dipped in tar, and hung by chains along the Thames River. For years it served as a warning to all would-be pirates.

Captain Avery and his finest prize, the Great Mogul's ship.

John "Long Ben" Avery

John "Long Ben" Avery was born near Plymouth, England, and began his career as a pirate at the age of 20 when he led a mutiny. Avery took command of the Spanish privateer *Duke* in Cadiz Bay, Peru.

The captain and six loyal crewmen were set adrift; the Jolly Roger was run up; and Avery set sail for the Isle of May. He stormed the town and held the governor as a hostage until he received the supplies he needed. Then he headed for Africa, plundering three British ships en route.

After filling his holds with slaves, Avery headed for America. But many of the slaves died on the way, and at the Island of Princes Avery seized two Danish slave ships. Now his trip was a complete success.

Next Avery sailed for Madagascar where he joined forces with the pirates Misson and Tew. Sailing off the Arabian coast they spied some ships from the fleet of the Great Mogul, ruler of India. The pirates gave chase. A broadside from one of the Mogul's ships killed the pirate Tew, and put his ship out of action. But the other two pirate ships quickly captured the *Fateh Mohamed* and the *Gunsway* with the Mogul's daughter aboard.

A pirate crew splits up its booty. (Painting by Howard Pyle)

Imagine Avery's surprise when his men carried up from the *Gunsway's* hold 200 bags containing 100,000 pieces of eight, solid gold plates and tankards, and dozens of diamonds, one as big as an egg. The total value of the cargo was over $2,000,000 — the largest pirate treasure ever.

The Great Mogul demanded Avery's capture. England offered a 500-pound reward for each member of his crew. The East India Company offered 1,000 pounds for each pirate. Avery couldn't stay in the Indian Ocean, and he couldn't sail for England. So he returned to America.

Avery buried some treasure at Gallop's Island and Pullen Point before sailing into Boston harbor. He stayed there until he thought it was safe to return to England. When he reached Bristol, Avery had over two million dollars in diamonds on him; yet he died a beggar only a few years later, tricked out of his money by illegal diamond merchants.

"Blackbeard"

Edward "Blackbeard" Teach was a giant of a pirate, standing six feet four inches and weighing 250 pounds. He wore a huge beard braided with pieces of hemp which he burned to cover his head in a frightening cloud of smoke. Blackbeard looked and acted like the Devil. He wore six pistols strapped to his chest, and could handle a 10-pound cutlass as if it were a duelling sword.

At first, he sailed under the pirate Jack Hornigold. Then Hornigold, fearing Blackbeard, gave him a ship of his own, the *Queen Anne's Revenge*. (Many pirates named their ships the *Revenge* or the *Adventure*.)

Blackbeard the Pirate, two versions.

The little horns protruding from his head are lighted matches.

Within a year, Blackbeard's one ship had grown to a small fleet menacing all shipping in the Bahamas. In 1718, England sent Woodes Rogers with a fleet of ships to get rid of the pirates. He offered them a pardon or the gallows. Many pirates accepted the pardon, but not Blackbeard.

He sailed for the Carolinas to establish his new base in Pamlico Sound. En route he took nine ships outside of Charleston harbor. He even took the ship of another pirate, Stede Bonnet. After secretly agreeing to split his booty with the governor of North Carolina, Blackbeard raided every ship that entered Pamlico Sound.

Finally, the governor of Virginia offered a reward of 100 pounds for Blackbeard, dead or alive. On November 17, 1718, two ships sailed against him under Lieutenant Robert Maynard, HMN.

At Pamlico Sound, Blackbeard had been celebrating his latest victory by announcing he was in league with the Devil. To prove it, he dragged his crew below deck, filled a room with burning brimstone, and laughed while the others choked on the smoke. Then, in a drunken rage, he shot off the kneecap of his first mate.

"If I don't kill somebody now and then," he roared, "you'll forget who I am."

By the time Blackbeard was aroused from his drunken stupor, the mouth of the sound had been blocked by Maynard's two ships. The first attacking ship hit a hidden sandbar. Blackbeard moved in to deliver a devastating broadside when a sudden change in wind grounded him too. Just as he got free, the second ship attacked. Blackbeard's cannon roared, and when the smoke cleared, the only Virginians left on deck were Maynard and his helmsman.

With a whoop, the pirates jumped onto the helpless ship — only to discover Maynard had fooled them. From below deck charged a swarm of slashing, shooting sailors. The pirates fought back, but they were greatly outnumbered. Soon only Blackbeard was left.

Blackbeard's Last Fight, a painting by Howard Pyle.

He had fought his way to the helm where Maynard was waiting for him. With one slash of his cutlass, he broke Maynard's sword in two. Maynard fired his pistol point-blank at Blackbeard, but it barely slowed him down. He knocked Maynard to the ground and raised his cutlass to deliver the final blow.

Suddenly a sailor hit him from behind with a heavy pike. Blackbeard roared like a wounded lion and turned to meet his attacker. Again the man hit him. Blackbeard staggered. Maynard grabbed a rapier lying on the deck and lunged at him. Blackbeard struck back. A bullet hit him, and then another. Yet Blackbeard refused to go down. He stood his ground, sailors all around him, fighting to the end. When he finally fell, there were 25 wounds in his lifeless body.

Jean Lafitte

The last of the great pirates was the Frenchman, Jean Lafitte (zhan leh-FEET). Around 1809, when the U.S. Army had only 6,000 men, Lafitte had over 1,000 pirates under his command. Lafitte's stronghold was in the swamps of Barataria, only 50 miles south of New Orleans. From there, he controlled the mouth of the Mississippi River and much of the Gulf of Mexico.

Lafitte attacked ships of all nations, killing their entire crews ("Dead men tell no tales") and sinking them. Finally, in 1810, Governor Claiborne of Louisiana formed a coast guard of 40 men and a few ships to try to stop him.

First Lafitte laughed at them. Then he cursed them. He was captured smuggling his booty into the city. The booty was probably from the American ship *Independence* which Lafitte had sunk that day. And this time there was a survivor to "tell the tale." Captain Williams had hidden under a sail when the pirates captured and set fire to his ship. As it sank into the sea, he jumped into the water and grabbed a piece of flotsam. A passing ship picked him up and brought him to New Orleans to testify against Lafitte.

Jean Lafitte (1782-1854)

Everyone in the city awaited the trial, except Lafitte. The day after his capture, he escaped to Barataria. The governor offered $500 for Lafitte's capture. Lafitte offered $1,500 for the governor's capture.

A force was being organized to attack Barataria when the War of 1812 began. The governor wanted to crush the pirates before they could join forces with the British; but now the men couldn't be spared.

On September 2, 1814, a British man-o-war sailed into Barataria with an offer for Lafitte. They wanted help in attacking New Orleans. In return, they would give him $30,000, a captaincy in the British army, and a pardon for all his men.

But Lafitte hated the English. So he delayed giving them an answer and sent word to Governor Claiborne. Lafitte warned of the coming attack and offered to help defend New Orleans.

The Americans replied with cannon fire. On September 11, Commodore Patterson attacked Barataria with six ships. Instead of dealing with the pirates, they had decided to destroy them.

Lafitte and most of his men escaped into the swamps. The Americans were left to defend New Orleans by themselves — 1,000 poorly armed men against 12,000 crack British soldiers, veterans of the Napoleonic wars.

When Andrew Jackson arrived to defend the city, he asked for Lafitte's help. He got it. When the battle of Villiere plantation began on December 23, 1814, Lafitte's pirates were in America's front lines.

The British attacked. And the British retreated. They had lost 700 men; the Americans had lost 31.

Before the British could rally their men for a second attack, a heavy fog rolled in. Out of the American lines came the Tennessee riflemen and the pirates. Creeping silently through the tall grass and ditches, they picked off the British soldiers one by one — only to disappear when reinforcements came.

It was January 8 before the British could attack again. And once again the pirate cannon roared, the Tennessee rifles barked. The British lost 2,600 troops; only 13 Americans were killed. New Orleans had been saved.

Lafitte was a hero, though not for long. In the spring of 1817, he set sail with a hand-picked crew for Port au Prince, Santo Domingo, hoping to establish a new pirate port. But the citizens of Port au Prince drove him away.

Lafitte settled on Galveston Island and for a short while he regained his previous power. But, when word of his piracies reached Louisiana, American gunboats were sent to drive him from the island. Lafitte and his men left without a fight, never again to anchor in an American port. Legend has it that he died some years later in Yucatan.

Pirate Treasure

With the death of Lafitte, the golden age of piracy came to an end. But the story doesn't end there. It lives on in tales of sunken treasure ships and buried booty.

According to legend, whenever pirates buried treasure, they killed one of their own crew and buried him with the booty so his spirit would guard it. But this hasn't frightened off the treasure seekers.

In the last 300 years, millions of dollars in treasure have been found, and it is believed that on the Atlantic coast alone, another 40 million awaits the adventurous. Maybe you'll be the one to discover Captain Kidd's treasure, or "Long Ben" Avery's.

You won't be the first to find pirate treasure. In 1962, a group of men found three million dollars in 10 Spanish ships that had been wrecked off the coast of Florida over 250 years ago.

Recently, underwater excavations began on the sunken pirate city of Port Royal, Jamaica. It was the "wickedest and richest city in the world" in its day. Then on June 7, 1692, a great earthquake hit the city, and in the words of one survivor:

> ... I never heard, nor could anything in my opinion appear more terrible to the eye of man: here a company of people swallowed up at once; there a whole street tumbling down; and in another place the trembling earth opening her ravenous jaws, let in the merciless sea so that this town is becoming a heap of ruins ...

The city sank, taking with it over 2,000 lives, and millions in pirate treasure. Much of it is still there. Fishermen claim that on a clear day you can see the roofs of the houses on the ocean bottom, and hear the ghostly tolling of the old church bells. And from somewhere down below, they say, comes a sound like 2,000 pirates singing:

> *Fifteen men on a dead man's chest . . .*
> *Yo-ho-ho and a bottle of rum*
> *Drink and the Devil had done for the rest . . .*
> *Yo-ho-ho and a bottle of rum.*

The Pull Ahead Books

AMERICA'S FIRST LADIES
    1789 to 1865

AMERICA'S FIRST LADIES
    1865 to Present Day

FAMOUS SPIES

SINGERS OF THE BLUES

WESTERN LAWMEN

WESTERN OUTLAWS

PRESIDENTIAL LOSERS

PIRATES AND BUCCANEERS

FAMOUS CRIMEFIGHTERS

We specialize in publishing quality books for young people. For a complete list please write

LERNER PUBLICATIONS COMPANY

241 First Avenue North, Minneapolis, Minnesota 55401